LUNCH BOX Laughs

Tony & Mike Nappa

D1568200

Standard Publishing
Cincinnati, Ohio

For Amy, who still doesn't know
when to laugh.

Standard Publishing, a division of Standex International Corporation, Cincinnati, Ohio.
© 2000 by Nappaland Communications, Inc. All rights reserved.
Bean Sprouts™ and the Bean Sprouts design logo are trademarks of Standard Publishing.
Printed in the United States of America.
Project editor: Lise Caldwell. Design: Diana Walters. Typesetting: Andrew Quach.

07 06 05 04 03 02 01 00   5 4 3 2

ISBN 0-7847-1064-3

A Note to Parents

Funny thing happened on the way to school the other day. Well actually, it happened the night before. My wife, Amy, was just finishing up the packing of our son's lunch.

"I need a joke," she said to me—an unusual occurrence because she's made a point of NOT laughing at so many of my otherwise hilarious funnies.

"Why?" I responded, thereby revealing my lack of insight into the human condition.

"You know how I always put a note on Tony's napkin and pack it in his lunch? Well a long time ago, I ran out of things to say, so I started writing jokes I knew on the napkin instead. Now I'm all out of jokes, so I need a joke."

I, in my husbandly helpfulness, proceeded to tell her an astonishingly funny joke—something about paint and the color green. When I finished, she simply sighed and said, "Never mind. I think I know where a joke book is downstairs."

Never one to be deterred, I started joining in that little napkin ceremony, making up corny jokes to share with my son. He, being an excellent judge of funny-ness (unlike his mother), liked them. In fact, he liked them so much, he decided to make up his own.

Before long, there was a full-fledged joke contest going on in my home, with both my son and me spouting witticisms and jockeying for that coveted "Funniest Person in the House" award. Then, Tony did the unthinkable: he got a joke published, the little stinker! With that he firmly grasped the coveted award—and had the press clippings to prove it.

Well, I thought, if you can't beat 'em, join 'em. So I recruited Tony and together we pooled our napkins . . . I mean jokes, and have now produced this little tome of mirth and merriment for you and your children.

You'll notice that the pages of this book are perforated. That's because we figured you too will be packing a child's lunch and suddenly need a joke. When that happens, simply tear out your favorite joke in this book and slip it in with the PB&J sandwich.

When your youngster opens lunch at school later that day, he will be treated (we hope) with an astonishingly funny joke! (Remember, a groan is as good as a laugh.) And you'll be treated to the satisfaction of knowing you planted a bright spot in your child's day. God gives us the gift of laughter. If we give that gift to our kids, we will have enriched their lives tremendously.

So what are you waiting for? Isn't it time to pack a lunch?

What do you get when you cross a dog and a praise song?

Why did the cats run away from the campground?

What do you get when you cross an apple with a parakeet?

What do you get when you cross a poodle with an ice cube?

A pup-sicle!

What do you get when you cross a bee with a flashlight?

What did page 140 say to page 141?

What should you do
if your hamburger
is losing a race?

Give it a little ketchup!

Why did the chef have to chase after his breakfast?

What do you get when you cross a dog with a number?

What do you call a preacher with torn clothes?

How do you keep an elephant from playing your piano?

Why did the girl throw an ice remover out the window?

What do you call a dachshund that's driving a sports car?

What do they serve in the salvage yard cafeteria?

Junk food!

Why did the baseball player throw cookie dough in the stands?

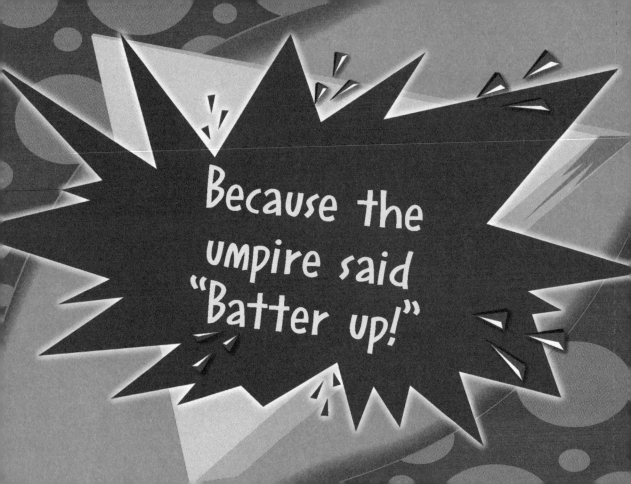

Why are bowlers bad baseball players?

What do you call a car made completely out of orange rinds?

An automopeel!

Why did Silly Sam bring a chair home from school?

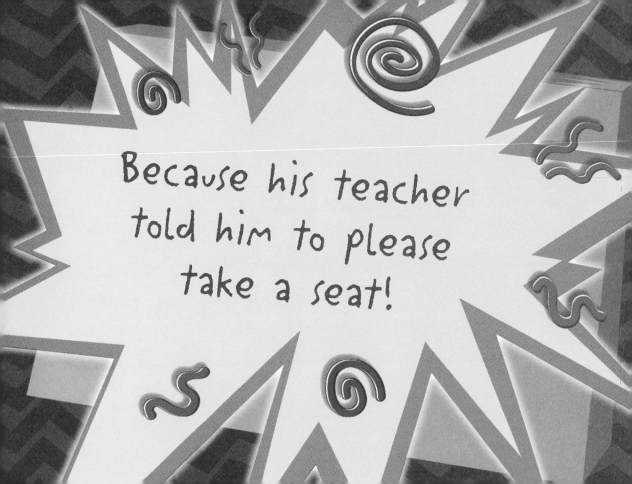

How can you
tell if a camera
is scared?

By its shutters!

What kind of camera does a chicken use?

Why did Amy throw her mom's credit card out the window?

Why did Mike take a leash into a thunderstorm?

Why did the camera have to go to jail?

Why did Tony buy
a cowboy hat
and boots?

What do you call a cat with eight legs?

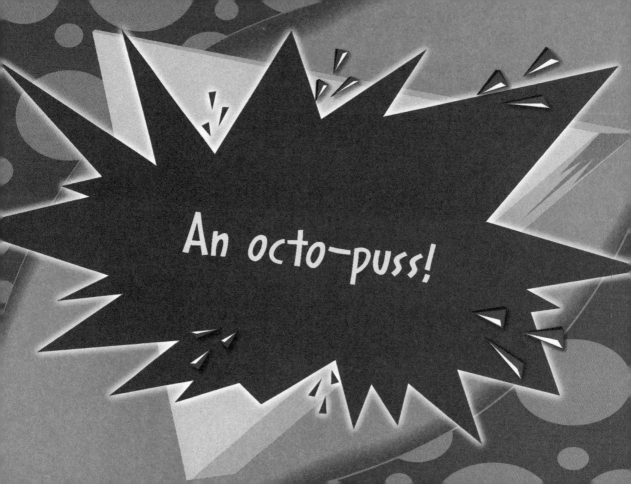

Why did Mike run across the intersection?

Why did the girl put a horse on her head?

What do you get when you cross a rodent and a chapel?

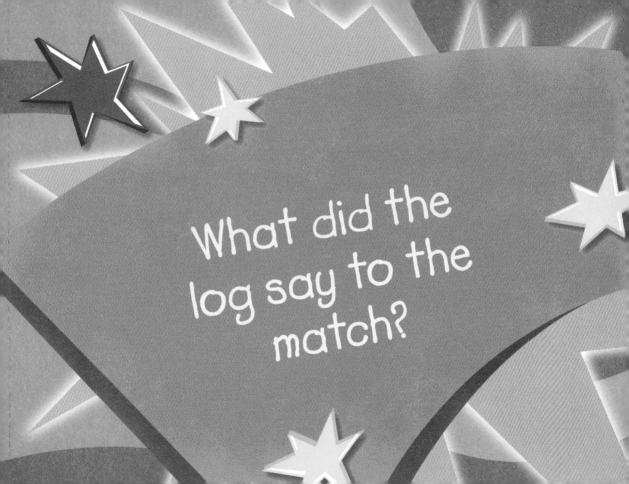

What did the log say to the match?

Why did the detective eat dinner at a restaurant?

Why did the boy throw banana cream out the window?

He was hungry for pie in the sky!

Why did the man put on his jeans and then dive out the window?

What do you call a flower that refuses to make dinner?

What do sharks
take to school
for lunch?

Why did the woman throw her book in the ocean?

Why is it a bad idea to give basketball players drinks out of your water glass?

What do you call a fruit that delivers a sermon?

What kind of bug likes to go to church?

A praying mantis!

What do you get when you bake stones with your bread dough?

Where did the skateboard go for Chinese food?

What do you call a sleeping Tyrannosaurus Rex?

A dino-snore!

What do you call it when a Triceratops takes out the trash?

What do you get when you cross a fish with Swiss cheese?

What do you call a Siamese kitten that's eating an ice cream cone?

What do you call a hen
that finishes first
in a race?

A quick chick!

What happens when you mix ice cream with homework?

How did the church label its restrooms?

What do you call a cob with only one kernel on it?

A uni-corn!

How can you tell if a unicorn has been in your freezer?

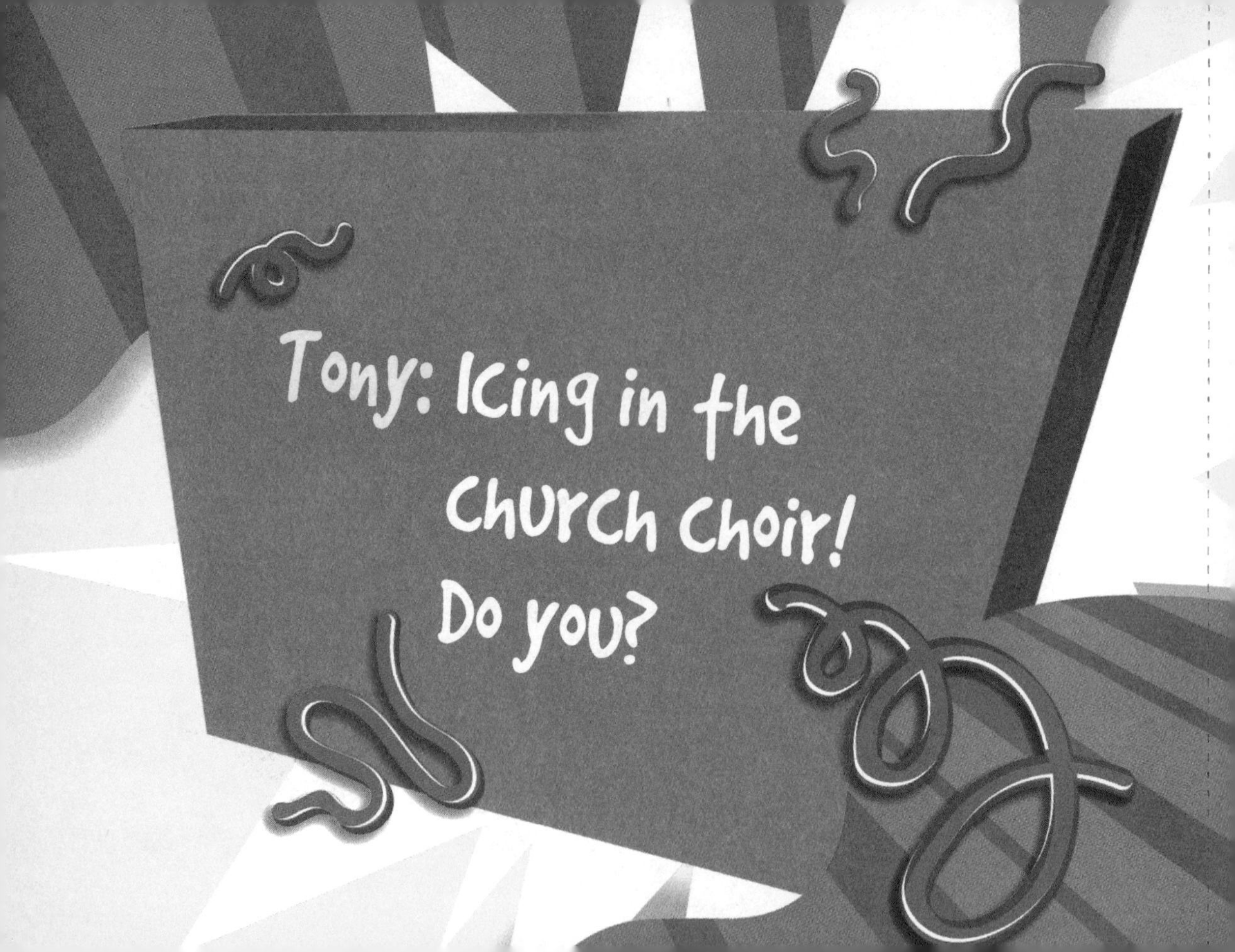
Tony: Icing in the church choir!
Do you?

Tony: Knock! Knock!
Mike: Who's there?
Tony: Ice cream.
Mike: Ice cream who?

Tony: Knock! Knock!
Mike: Who's there?
Tony: Disguise.
Mike: Disguise who?

Tony: Knock! Knock!
Mike: Who's there?
Tony: Kenya.
Mike: Kenya who?

Tony: Kenya loan me a dollar? I wanna get a candy bar!

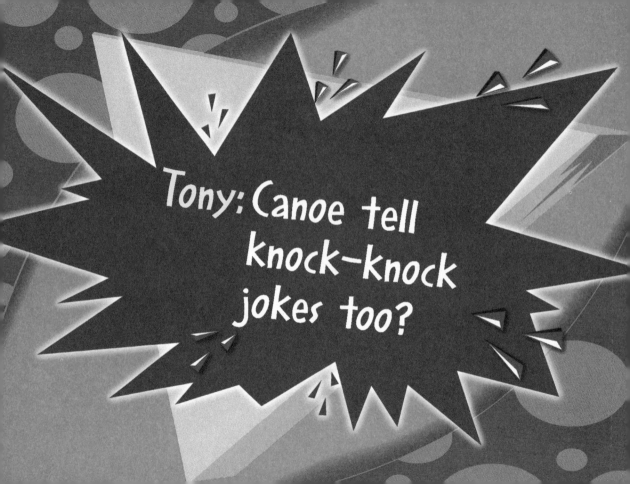

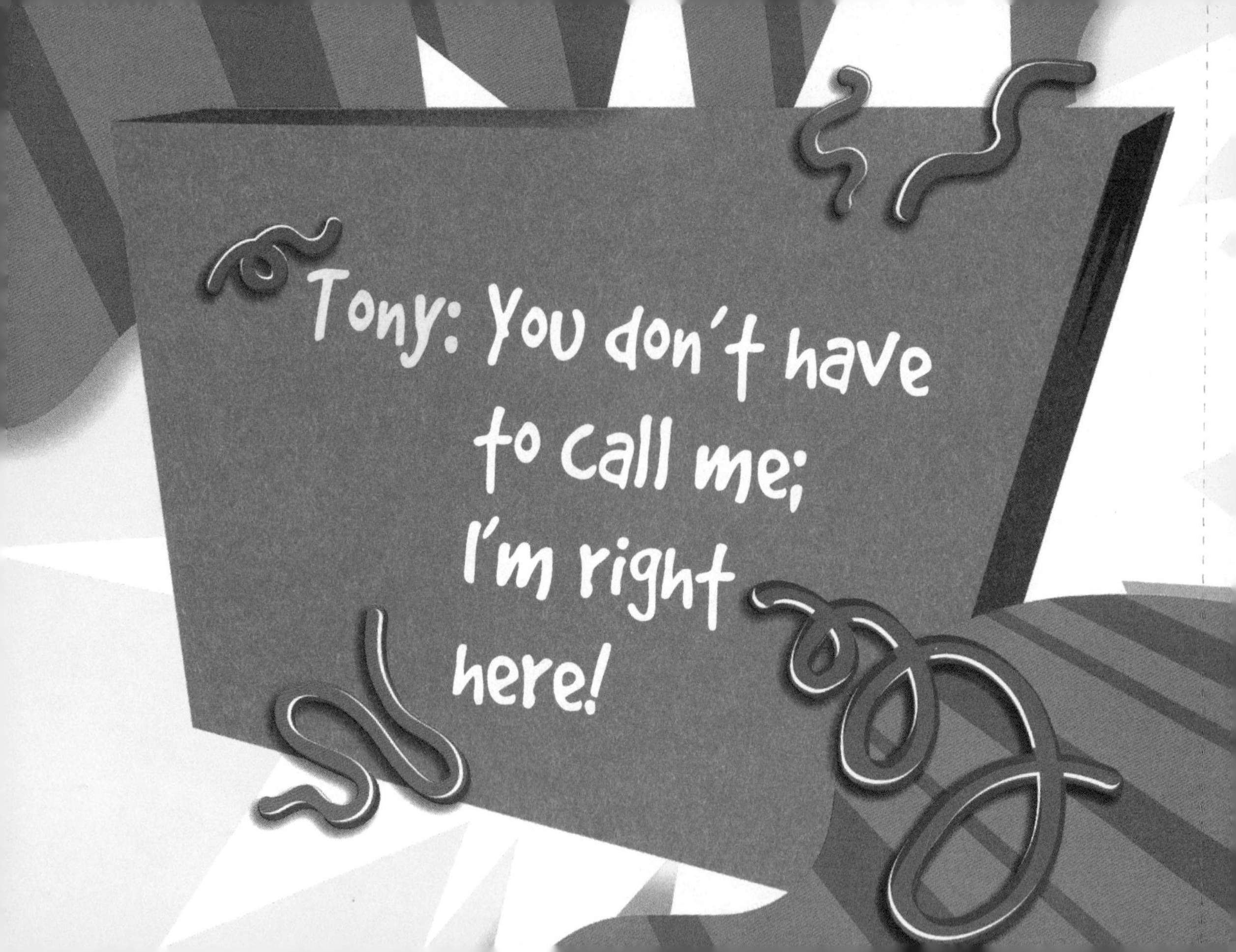
Tony: You don't have to call me; I'm right here!

Tony: You don't have to cheer, it's only a knock-knock joke!

What did the preacher say to the salad?

How do you keep the king of spades from knocking over your card house?

Deck him!

What did the leopard say when the hunter saw him running across the plain?

Why did the baseball player have to go to jail?

Why did the baseball player leave the bowling alley in the middle of a game?

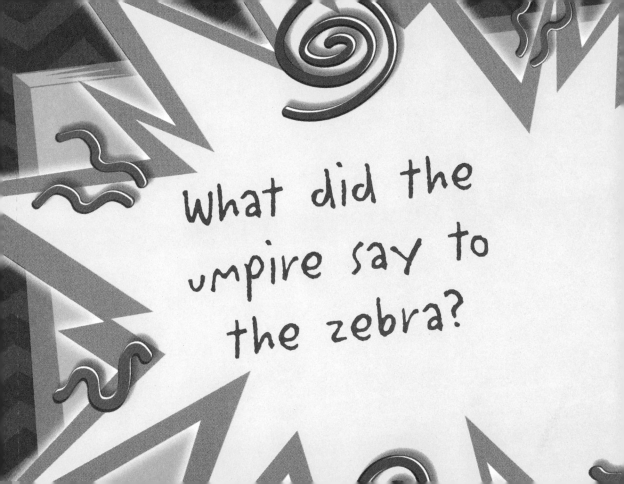

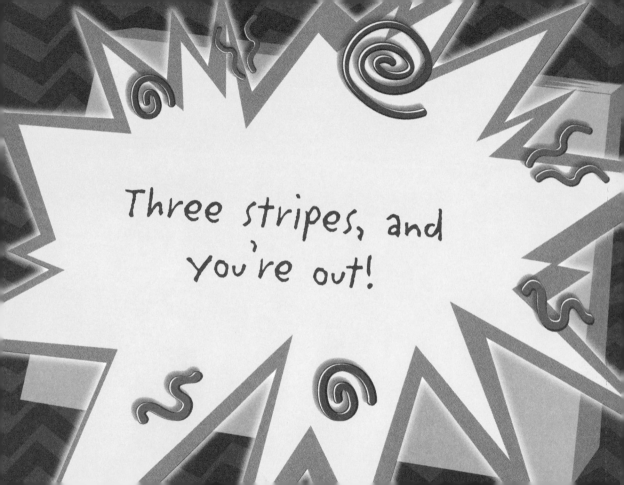

What do you call a monkey that wins a chess tournament?

A chimp champ!

What do you call a mallard that wins the lottery?

Why did Tony take his clock on the bus?

He wanted to see time travel!

Why did Amy take her clock to the park?

What do skunks like best about church?

What kind of horse likes to sneak up on you in the dark?

A night mare!

What do you get when you place two toddlers in the same room as a spinning toy?

What should you do
if a baseball
insults you?

What should you do if you see a few minutes on the street?

Take five!

Why did the cowboy throw his revolver out the window?

Why did the baseball player throw his girlfriend in the air?

Why did Mike
put his bed under a
meteorologist's map?

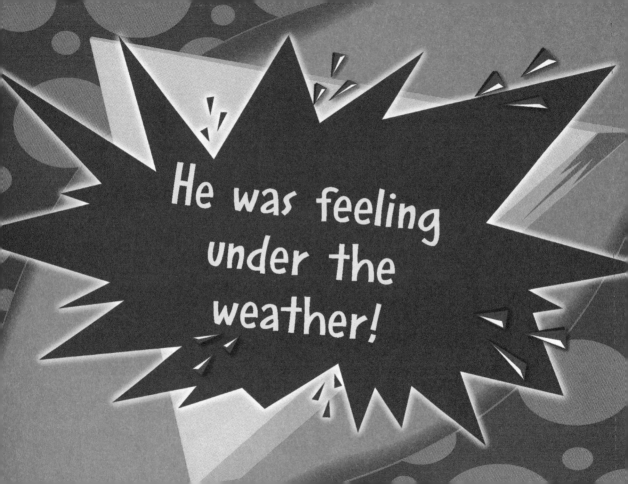

Why did the bank teller throw his gloves at the ceiling?

Because the
bank robber said,
"Put your hands
in the air!"

What do you get when you cross an airplane, a pair of glasses, and Sir Lancelot?

A jet-eye knight!